Uninvited Feelings

Thank You For Your Support
Ms. Scott.

Ron M. Kelly

Uninvited Feelings

A Book of "Thought Poetry"

Keenan Kelly

Writers Club Press
San Jose New York Lincoln Shanghai

Uninvited Feelings
A Book of *"Thought Poetry"*

Writers Club Press
an imprint of iUniverse, Inc.

For information address:
iUniverse, Inc.
5220 S. 16th St., Suite 200
Lincoln, NE 68512
www.iuniverse.com

Any resemblance to actual people and events is purely coincidental. This is a work of fiction.

ISBN: 0-595-22266-8

Printed in the United States of America

First and foremost I dedicate this book to God who is most important in my life. Secondly, this book is dedicated with the greatest love and affection to my family and friends for their love, support and encouragement.

Contents

II.. THOUGHTS FOR THE MIND

Contents

III.. UNINVITED FEELINGS

IV.. ANOTHER CONVERSATION

Contents

Acknowledgements

I would like to thank the wonderful people who provided me the needed feedback and the confidence to share my thoughts. I'm blessed to have individuals in my life that understand my vision. At this time I want to thank you for sharing your time with me and for allowing me to share my thoughts with you.

In memory of my grandfathers, the late Dewitt Hall and Emmitt Kelly, who always believed in me.
"Beauty is often a decision based upon a judgment rendered by one's eyes or one's heart."
"Love is often a decision based on a judgment rendered by one's heart or one's mind."

Keenan M. Kelly

Introduction

Humbly, do I welcome you to my world of thoughts. Thoughts that track me down while understanding my search for words. Thoughts that hold my hands close to my heart as I give life to the silence that lives within me. My thought poetry is a mind conceived idea which languages feelings in descriptive words with hope that enjoyment might be provided to all who would share my world of thoughts.

Keenan Kelly

I.. Gracious

I Drown In Your Eyes

I've not yet learn to swim
Thus the reason
When I look into your eyes I drown
Only to be rescued by your angelic smile
My spirit latches tightly to your rosy lips
Making my tongue spill—all that is in my heart
A flood of desire to love you

The sunlight dances and shimmers
Upon the calm water—across this new found ocean of
    urge
The ache of my cry is for forgiveness
To my submerged hope which has been lost
As I swim in this breathtaking love I've found
Her smile gives me strength and courage
While I look into the pool of her eyes
As I slowly and quietly drown

So tonight may you immerse in my passion
This tide of love I can no longer hide
May your lips give me the kiss of life
As I joyfully drown in your eyes

Kiss

I'm tempted by your lips—
For the mere touch of your lips upon mine
I would drink your kiss and become drunken by pleasure-
As though your lips contain droplets of wine

The sweetest taste of love I'm desiring—
A delicious body sensation—
I'm warned by the beauty in your eyes
That your lips are more than just a temptation

Your smile makes me feel—as though I'll burst inside
You've touched that secret place—I didn't know
My heart could open so wide

When your lips speak I become a prisoner
I'm captured by every word
Only to be released—each moment-
When my mind—desires the urge—

To quench my thirst-
Is by drinking your kiss
Having my tongue seek your love fountain
Bringing to life feelings I knew not could exist

I'm tempted by your lips
For the mere touch of your lips upon mine
Now I wish to take a sip
Of a kiss that would lose me in time

An Uneven Bronze Ballad

Oh Spain, could there be unheard love messages in your
    smile
The unyielding answers of why the eastward wind
    breathes gently towards me
Oh the beauty of Spain mutes my joy
And for her love I have gone to war and returned
    unharmed
How I have abandoned all fear of love—telling myself
    Spain receives me
She is an unconquered frontier—where the grassland
    grows pure and green
Though my courage is overshadowed by the ambers of
    the sun

I would like to lift the veil placed before my Spain
So that I might see behind the confined walls of her
    beauty
I want to place my fingers against all of Spain's flesh—
My touch has no sense of direction
The look of unreal softness is she—making me a spectator
    of her bronze skin
Oh Spain splendid is your beauty, which shines so bright
Making you the capital of my world

Majestic is the speaking of her name
Which elevates above all other nations
Oh Spain, how I love you—you are my country
That place I've never arrived at—will my heart ever know
    such lovely and fertile ground
Though the spread of refusal is not shown upon the face
    of my would be love
There is no welcoming shadow confessing its undying
    devotion toward my want
Oh Spain, tonight the sky is without stars because they
    hide in my soul
So that their tears for me are not seen

The lips of Spain move as if to call to me
Each word and every sound her sweet voice shall make
I shall string them together like pearls with my two hands
Yet I find this small labor in love totally in vain
Due to a lesson quickly taught revealing I'm a student
    slow to learn
Because unheard is this sparrow's voice
And my eyes only hear the beauty of her smile

Oh Spain out of your magnificent castle
Please see me not with your stained glass vision
But see me through your pure crystal windows
Therefore making crystallize moments more detailed
Oh Spain, I am like a seed in comparison to your
    loveliness
Yet everything I know about loving you is inside of me
Awaiting your sunshine of passion and your water of
    mercy
For you in your autumn robe of colors could share great
    things with me

Spain my beautiful bronze queen
Permit me so close to you that it stains my heart
That our union of eternity turns cobblestone pathways
    into life's serenity
The desperation heard in my plea mutes the silence

Birthing a prayer from the screams which have pierced
    the ears of heaven
Though love is not the answer felt in the unheard
    messages in your smile
May my eyes bury my love for you somewhere in the
    depths of your bronzed heart

An Opened Book

With so much love to give
Yet so much pain received
She vowed she would never love again

Unfortunately for me
Her heart has been deceived
And this was my beginning and end

Love in her eyes
Hate in her heart
Her story I know so well

Each turning of the page
I could feel her rage
Every word in such detail

If only I could absorb each tear she cried
And kiss away each ache she had

Bring closure to her suffering world
Chase away any thoughts that made her sad

Chapter one reads like a fairytale
A woman so full of life

A friend to some, a mom to others
And yes, to one a wife

By chapter three—I came to see
A lady in such turmoil

On the verge of divorce, crying till she's hoarse
Her every hour is a minute void

I seek for assurance that she'll be okay
As the page I slowly turn

Her past her teacher, her present her test
Her future will show what she has learned

Gracious

Lady, when it comes to you
The Lord doesn't condemn me
For he is merciful unto me
Please Lord, set me free
Offer unto me the peace due to me by your justifiable
    faith
Lady, am I mistaken by what I see
When I place my eyes upon you
The heavens bear witness to how you inspire me
I declare my feelings toward you
As though I am a man at war with love
I've opened my eyes and heart to things I've already
    known
So where is the discovery of things already shown?
Did love find me unprepared?
If so, should I have to suffer?
For my yearn to know true love intimately
To set expectations that love will not obey
Oh Lord, I put my trust in your tender mercy
And I make no demands on the Lady and her love
For pleasure does not lie in the end result
Lady,—graciously I accept the spiritual agreement
To accept love in it's perfect and imperfect stages

Picture Of Love

I think of you dear—lady
It seems like all the time
A vision of such beauty
Resting softly upon my mind

So when the hatred of the world
Tries to distort my precious view
I simply picture love
And my picture looks like you

Unseen Love

When I kissed the wind
My kiss landed upon your lips
You kissed the wind back
And from the sweetness of that kiss I slowly took a sip

I whispered secrets to the wind in hopes that no one
    would ever hear
My vows and promises, my hopes and dreams
Somehow reached your ear

I held out my arms to the wind
To hold it and by it to be held
It's breath rest softly upon my skin
Colorless beauty is the description the eyes do tell

My heart aches as I wait to see your face
I want to see the wind dancing in your hair
Silently and alone I wait
For the wind to answer my prayer

My anticipation of loving you—my wind—is only
    known by me
The wind is a carefree soul
A reminder that to cherish it
I must be willing to pay the fee

Yet if all my yesterdays become tomorrows
Before my love is known by you
May my spirit of love be felt
Every time the wind blows through

Garment Designer

Within my jaws my teeth sew together pieces of fabric
For the aftertaste of melted garments
Is ever so refreshing to the throats opening
Just a reminder that a dinner mint wipes away the thrill
The thrill of thoughts
Where her hips—wrapped in a fashion of love
Allow the curves of her body to design edible outfits
Where her breasts—seduces their stitches of restraint
For a sweet taste of freedom
I place my lips on unhidden buttons, which seek my
    attention
I run my fingers against the smooth silky pieces of cloth
Seemingly there is a quiver against my hands
Suddenly I have an urge to drape myself in this soft fabric
Enclose my being in the warmth of her apparel
Which is eager to undress me
The lips of zippers and straps bruised my tongue
Greeting me feverishly
Now the joining of attire exist no longer
Exposing the fleshy hidden treasures
Permitting my mouth to carefully massage this seamless
    dessert
Consenting to the consuming of all that she wears
And all that she bares
Then after devouring my desire
For all to see
I will simply wear the love of her garment
Like an ornament around my heart

Thy Kingdom Come

The letter from God
Instructs me on how I must protect my kingdom
For this shell of a house
My body
Is the temple in which
Thy spirit dwells
So wherever thy spirit is
I bring my kingdom
Therefore wherever my kingdom goes
Thy kingdom come

Thoughts That Smell

I smell you in my thoughts
Indicating even my thoughts have dreams
Somewhere in my mind—her love said hello
The relevance of her voice
Does not compare to the essence of her smile
Embracing me tenderly

Casting a fragrance of apple blossom days
Which fills my nostrils
Taking me back- to a closed eye scent
Fading yet still whole
Because I still smell you in my thoughts

Wings For Flight

Take me a caterpillar and make me a butterfly
Allow my wings to find moisture in broken leaves
May the river rocks brush away dust from my torn body
Against the stillness of the rocks—water throws itself
The two sing out of tune yet their song resonates in my
    soul

I stretch my newly formed wings toward the sun
And the sunrays speaks to my heart—while sedating my
    passion to fly
I'm mesmerized by the presence of the sky
I slowly sip on the taste of its beauty

Now mercy has found me
Resting itself upon the hills of my emotions
Massaging the exposed surface of my naked flesh
Strengthening my wings for flight
Peaceful is the touch of nature's hand

Absence the writing of words—a song is created everyday
My wings are giving power to dance
My flight becomes a thank you to a love
Which would take me a caterpillar and make me a
    butterfly

Peach

You live in my imagination
The sunset makes patterns of my thoughts
Tracing the ripe peach juice trail
Guiding my fingers across your lips
Toward your chin
Barely brushing the stickiness found on your neck
My tongue dances across your peach flesh
Desiring to praise the flesh discovered
Between your breasts and your mother's gift of life
I eat the sounds you slowly utter
Your words become the peach I nibble
Only to stop when I lick the fleshy covered sugar buds
The smile of the sunset's light falls upon us
Covering everything—my thoughts, my emotions
Unveiling your peeled back pleasure
Offering me an invitation to slip deeper
Into your peach world
Causing your flesh to melt into mine
Rewarding me a ride upon the clouds
For tonight you've become my fruit for life

Twisted Perception

My image is created and distorted
By what you've seen and read
I'm to be the unappreciated being of life
Not born but bred
I'm to be guilty until proven innocent
My every thought to be a crime
My body is to consume an unhealthy diet of violence and
      drugs
I'm to be a disgrace to mankind
By this I'm often reconnected with my past
And what my forefathers went through
I see in my dreams the blood spilled
To discredit the images which were not true
So when you look at me realize
That I represent this individual
Please let your mind slowly digest this
And do not hold me accountable for your image visual

The Bell Is Calling

There goes that bell again ringing in my ear
An everlasting sound to me
That I hear and hear and hear
The children are laughing and shouting
As if they all were deaf
My body is here with them
But my soul has packed and left

A Glowing Candle

May my love dream out loud
As I'm taken by the seductive blend
Of night and a glowing candle

Yet in the crackling of pains flame
Hides the remembrance of love
The heat reveals much yet it shares nothing

While the sensual touch of belonging
And the delightful aroma of peace
Simply float about in the emptiness of distance

My fragile heart walks above the flame
Allowing my curious eyes to search for a better tomorrow
Never expecting to find it

Because the melting of wax reminds me
I've been burned before
Now the soft kisses of my tears
Make smoke of a flame while silencing my dream

As my emotions become undone
Like the ashes, which lay at the foot
Of a once glowing candle

The Sole Of Your Heart

The sole of your heart is in comparison to the coolness of the day, which washes over me invading my sanctuary—the likeness of a sweet drink of water, which is alluring to the parchedness of my throat—requesting that I relish in the sugar found at the sole of your heart—

So Her Colors Never End

My heart reached out to her
As my eyes watched her cry
To prevent her from such hurt
That's what I wished inside

Could a moment in time
Bring about such pain
A love storm shower
Her tears used for rain

Every drop symbolizing
The love and truth within
Her smile will be the rainbow
Showing her hurt at an end

Freely as the rainbow shines
She shall love again
I'll take her heart in mine
So her colors never end

Unspoken

Your love sits on my tongue
Wonderfully touching me
Drifting in silence are my thoughts
In search of you—
In search of the last time I called your name
Because uncertain am I of the time between last we talked
You my love glide about my heart
Like smoke in the darkness
Watering my eyes—which feel no pain
May the flow of my tears say—what words leap to hear
May this untamed river introduce me to love
Without quenching the fire which uses passion as wood
Love from your lips is made lush and ripe to my ear
Causing me to hear the words "I love you" twice
For my tongue simply repeated
The echoing of your words to my tears
So when it comes to you—ocean engulfing is my cry
Never drowning is the unspoken sound
Of—I love you

The Attendant

Peculiar is my heart as I'm turned over to my passion
That passion which attends to your love
Allowing me to hear what you are feeling
My desire for you articulates
Your yet to be spoken thoughts
While eyes of the land stare at me as my voice splatters up
    against me
Oh your mouth is my oasis
The deepest river shows itself still
You are my river making my hands small
As I carry your lips to my mouth—this task expands time
Moments move backwards
Tumbling minutes roll down the hillside
Consuming my breath quietly—because I can't keep up
    with falling hours
I want to attend to your unworded ideas
May my heart enwrap your soul
Making the spirit you are cling to me as the sun does the
    sky
And though I have no crown to wear
It is the holding of your hand, which makes me king of
    the land
Please allow my heart to excavate fragments of love from
    the day
So that I may piece together a jewel so that all can see
Peculiar is my heart as I'm turned over to my passion
That passion which delights itself in you
And though I'm not perfect—I love you perfectly
For everything you are always brings me to you

Thus perfection is found in a peculiar passion
Which attends to love regardless of where and how it is
  found

Love's Blueprint

Let my love be your shelter
Make my heart your home
Let the openness of my world
Give your soul a place to roam

This home is built on trust
The foundation laid with my two hands
The walls are held together by honesty
And painted by a coat of give and take
So there are no demands

Each nail is covered by a kiss
To smooth away the sharp edges
We will lay a carpet of understanding
And hang paintings on our promises and pledges

So when you look out of the windows
It is my eyes you are looking into
In hopes that you make my heart your home
The door I've left open for you

A Lonesome View

I took for granted what seemed like trivial moments
Now I view them as monumental times
Never stopping to appreciate the simplicity of love
Feeling like that would exaggerate that which was mine
So obvious did I care—I thought
Ignorant was the world if it could not see
Yet, unnoticed went your easy wishes
Now without you—touching is the tenderness of your
  plea

In A Single Word

If in a single word
I could find the cure for your pain
That word I would speak
To remove the ache from your heart
Wipe away the tears your eyes do weep
From my lips to your ears- that word
Would be spoken often and clear
For your mind to understand—that which it did hear
My soul would choose to believe
As long as I could see you smile
That in a single word
Prayer brings about the greatest ease for a while

Captured Being

If you take my hand
Then you take my heart
If you take my heart
Then you take my mind
If you take my mind
Then you take my thoughts
If you take my thoughts
Then you take my feelings
If you take my feelings
Then you see my soul
But just remember
You've been told
That it seems so simple
Yet, it means so much
To take a being
With the start of just a touch

My Yellow Dressed Tulip

In my garden—a yellow tulip grows
As the sun beams downward—
Casting a long shadow on the soft earth
The sky tends to take pictures of my garden
Allowing the clouds invisible eyes—
To peak at the distance imagery—then quickly covering
    it up

The portrait of this tulip stains my heart
And with love engraves itself into my soul
Dragging my hands from the rich soil
So that I might reach for the heavens—
What cloud would desire to cover up such chiseled
    features?

Oh my tulip in this meadow of golden love
Charming my blood—kissing my stolen breath
Yellow petals talk as they blow in the wind
Casting sweet scents that leave floating memories

As night falls—my flower will soon fade away—
Hiding in my admiration of this garden
Hiding in my heart—
The place where my tulip will tomorrow bloom again
Oh my lady in her yellow dress
Giving beauty to my garden
For in the rich soil of my heart
She has planted the root of her love

Honor's Debt

I can never repay you for giving me the honor to love you
For it has been just that
An honor
To some I may have been unworthy
Of such an opportunity
To others I've enjoyed
An unearned moment in time

What's the cost?
This dream of love
I thought I richly deserved
A profit for only the world
The union of our heart and mind

My Mistake

Let me not speak so that your ears may hear
And have your mind not try to interpret
Let me speak to your heart for the sincerity of my words
It shall detect

For my want—
My need for your acceptance of me
Is stronger than
Your need and want to forgive me

I can't use my eyes to see myself
Therefore I must rely on others
Such as yourself—to show me
Who I am yet judge me not

Again it is your heart
My words hope to reach
But it will be your actions
Which answer my plea

I'll admit my hopes are slightly diminished
From living in an unforgiving world
Yet I can't deny
Still for you—I chose to care
Punishment for me seems unfair
For I've never taken a breath for granted
This pain alone I'm facing
And if loving you is a mistake
Then it is a mistake worth making

The Presentation

The presentation of your silent spirit
Captivates me
The strength of your unspoken spirit
Bounds my being
For the language of your quiet spirit
Is written beautifully upon my heart
What evil or pain would dare confront
The silence of your spirit

For your walk represents all that is good
Soft steps you take
The sweet power of your silent spirit
Revealing the inner beauty within
Pleasing the world outside
Giving faith and hope a chance
The presentation—your silent spirit
Delighting itself in abundance

Gabriella

Like a pendulum—swings the throbbing of my heart
For Gabriella my air does breathe—
Her beauty envying the midnight stars
Even the sky takes a bended knee
Gabriella, her silhouette of beauty
Commanding I sit at her feet
I'm a lover of her voice, which sings
Love songs in my heart as I sleep
Her songs call to me—swaying me to dance
I leap at each note that I hear
Bruised bones applaud in stance
Each song is sweeter than the song before
Soaring higher at each note I hear
Rivers run forever loving pure
Her every note is crystal clear
My heart is attentive to this vision of love
Gabriella- my composer of joy
Irreplaceable is her sheet of music
Mute emotions kiss sounds that roar
Gabriella, my eyes swallow your tender skin
Woman how beautiful you are to me
My love will be the theme song tonight
For in my heart Gabriella's song—is why I sleep

Composed Outwardly

The slow music of a single violin
Strings together the chords which produces love's life
The elegance of its spirit
Takes hold of my soul as if to break me
Oh this violin—the seductress of my heart
Allows me to find my dignity
While losing my composure over loving you
May my tears say what mumbled words can't
I pray your ears will make perfect
My cry entangled in a love speechless of words

Once again the violin's music searches within me
And yes the bow did point my feet
To the middle of a golden meadow
Near the still pond—where the wild flowers grow
Where inside of me the music finds a harvest of promises
Broken, blooming, dying
Allowing me to find memories of you in my attempt to
    forget you
Oh how the music plays

This music is born under the white moon
Each note cradles my heart
While arousing my feelings
While composing me for a new day
For the single violin knows
That I control my love for you like the wind
And like the day of death—love controls me
As the violin sings to me the last sweet notes of a once
    known love

Tonight The Rain Cries
(I Miss You)

The rain cries because it now understands
How the familiar scent of you
Which spreads itself like morning dew
Wounds my muffled memories

Understood is a once forgotten fragrance
How it rips at my heart—
Unhidden are my chocolate covered secrets of pain
The shadows of the dark now bloom like apple orchards

How I regret given rest to the beautiful springtime
    thoughts
Like worker bees your scent is once again forever busy
Making sweet nectar of our long ago laughter

With gloved hands I want to remove my conscious mind
For succulent juices drench my soul
As your scent is freshly squeezed all over me again

Powerless am I to escape the air
Which carries your fragrance like broken tears
Reminding my face why my hands are also wet
For my weeping is the voice heard in the forest
Whenever voiceless rain cries tears

And tonight it smells like rain

Man Made

I've woven my hands around your waist
So as not to get lost in you
As I dig a tunnel from your eyes to your parted lips
Like a slender ocean wave—is the movement of your hips
Then without moving we dance
Oh the mouth of your island grows thirsty for me
So I spread myself thinly across your earth
While following the light that shines inside of you
There I hide from distance sorrow
Which does not spare me—forcing me onward
I whisper deeply as I climb between the borders that
     surround your island
My breath slides across your sensitive and allusive skin
I find pleasure in the texture of your earth
Your fields and gardens are beyond one's sight—
So I follow my hands down a slope not afraid of what I
     might find
I admire the endearing landmarks
That lay so remarkable upon your grounds
Your island's landscape tends to kiss my fingers
The request to stay is felt but I must not obey
I must swim, walk, and run back to your thighs
Across your neck, down your shoulders, out of your navel
I must find your waist
Now I imagine not loving your land
I imagine not remembering the island you offered to me
Only to find myself unable to forget

II.. Thoughts For The Mind

Johnny

Where Johnny laid two years ago
Was marked by a heavy rust stain
A mother still prays for Johnny though
Because it does more than ease her pain

Johnny was a good child
Trouble free he seemed to be
But death in a rage so wicked and wild
Took away our beloved Johnny

Some say it was a shot to his head
Others say a stab to the heart
Silence becomes the way of the dead
Only life knows the exited part

I can still hear his mother's scream
Even though I close my eyes when I do
Her tears seem to have made a stream
As she cried out "Johnny, I love you"

So Lord, if you can hear me
And God, I know you can
Take care of my son Johnny
As I become a forgiving man

Loveless Hands

As I held her hands, and gave her a hug
I knew hate was the reason for which I loved
My war with pain, a sea of tears
My heart scarred by a woman for so many years
Trying to hate her for who she was
But only to love her and only because
At birth she held me her touch I felt
For her hands were cold as her eyes well wept
I've hated the world and have longed to say
Woman of my birth be carried away
So we speak our hellos as if saying goodbye
We touch, time freezes and we both know why
She is my mother and my mind understands
Now no hate in my heart, but still no love in her hands

Time's Hourglass Shape

Time's hourglass shape curves
Around my elbow's distance yesterday
Tomorrow's forever shares with me
A bowl of dry leaves
Causing my mouth to speak unwritten chapters
Of a history's continuation to collect dreams
In packed boxes stored within shelved minds
Only pen and paper sharp enough to slice open
The harden tears, the undetected whispers
Wiping the residue on decaying leaves
Can truly bend the past's dusty body
Making real the intelligence of sand
That falls within time's hourglass shape

Look Over Bay

The mellow sound of the rushing water
The ravishing beauty of "Look Over Bay"
The warmth and softness of her breath
As she pleaded, "Please stay"
The snowy white sand that played upon the beach
The pebbles, and the blue-sky added touch
The soft sounding water waves in our background
I wonder if she was asking too much
The moon was bright this unpredictable night
The stars seemed to watch our every move
There she was "the extreme beauty"
And the night knew what we planned to do
An event that was never played
Upon this virgin sand
Now stood a woman, now stood a man
The exuberant life that exploded between them
Is never to be described
The moment that took place lives on
And that night shall never die

Lady Are You Proud Of Me

Lady, are you proud of me
Of all the things I've done
Locked behind these bars
A jail cell is what I've become

Lady, all your prayers and tears
I guess you feel were in vain
My fate was the jail cell
My wish was no more pain

Lady, I often think of you
And the dreams you had for me
But the cell envisioned something else
Please accept our apology

Lady, if you can hear my voice
My cry is like no other
Yes, the jail cell raised your son
But lady, you are the greatest mother

Mother Of Two

A mother kneeled and prayed
As she had done every night before
I'm a mother of two
Two sons, two jobs and a body well too weak for much
   more

Lord my prayer goes out to the needy and less fortunate
   than I
Two sons, two jobs and a body too weak but we will make
   it by and by

Father, as I hold to your unchanging hand
Knowing your name will remain the same
Two sons, two jobs and a body too weak for tears to be
   contained

The struggle I face in my everyday life, seems more than
   I can bear
Two sons, two jobs and a body so weak
Though I know how much you care

Well I've taken up enough of your time
But I wanted to say thank you
For two sons, two jobs and the gift of your love
Which strengthens this body on through

When My Will — Will Not

When my will—will not
Lord, I think of you
When I can yet can't
Pray is what I do
When what I know is unknown
In you Lord, I do believe
And when I'm brave from fear
Lord, thank you for what I've achieved
Now when I do and don't
Because Lord, it's your right and wrong
I hope I've been good enough
When you call your angels home

Nameless Love

I had a private conversation
With you in my mind
My silly thoughts made you smile
I seem so brilliant at times
The silence tends to comfort me
Bringing me closer to you
Irreversible is this moment
Every thought—a dream come true
The loving distance between
My eyes to your lips
Measures the boundless passion
Outlining the thoughts of a relationship
Your smile holds my heart
Your eyes kiss my soul
This incomplete romance
Leaving me a dear thought to hold
Yes, I feel more than I can see
While I'm attempting to understand
This private conversation
With this faceless woman

Casting Visions

Love's imagination moves around the moon ten times
Casting visions on the sun
Kissing the sky's spine
Whispering to the souls of lovers
So not to tell their secrets
While the lightly fallen dew on brows
Echoes loudly without a voice
Elusive sensations express notions of love
That is to lovers delightfully unexpected
Awakening a soul whose dormant heart
Blooms from newfound joy
The wind softly breathes on the skin
While it's colorless fingertips slowly massages the mind
Love's imagination moves around the moon one time
Casting visions on the sun
Kissing the boundless sky's spine

Lord I Do

No beauty in words
Or in phrases I speak
If I cannot say it is of the Lord I speak

No beauty in vision
Or wanting thereof
If I cannot see it is the Lord I love

No quality in time
Or in years gone pass
If I cannot make—Lord your will my task

So from this day forward Lord I place you first
Because everything else has little worth

Finding Water

The unknowns in my life would like to be forgotten
While unused love weeps guilty tears
As grief swells up inside of me like a newly dug spring
The maturing of the day causes me to make the grass my
  bed
Yes, the springtime grass has awaken after its long winter
  sleep
Giving hope for love to all who would share in the fantasy

I lay down not to sleep but to think
Thus the reason I make the day my mattress
Because it forms to the words of my thoughts
I've been induced beyond the birth of love—in a thought
Here I create a language which allow mountains and
  hillsides
To outline unknown speech
My mind and heart become bed covering for all that is
  within me

My speech listens to my words and my voice stares at me
As if to validate the world I live in
What value is the discovery of language?
If my words do not kiss your lips while being softly
  whispered in your ear
Unattractive are my findings as it relates to love's
  unshared lips
A touch, which knows my desire and caresses not my
  want of pleasure
My thirst finds no water

Now with night upon me—I'm distracted by the beauty
    of love
To me it is so endearing
Love please hear me and make yourself accessible to me
Letting your passion be your influence
Ravishing thoughts of you rearranged the pillows under
    my head
Not allowing me to sleep
So I sit in the crescent moon and swing back and forth
To a love song in my soul

I know soon my hands will write of you the way I see you
My heart will love you the way I feel the need to love
And then my thirst will be quenched—without ever
    tasting your passion of love words
Thus the reason the unknowns in my life would like to be
    forgotten

The Nape Of My Neck

She peels away my emotions
Though I'm petals of a carnation
Scented is the touch of her fingers
Carving a hollow spot
Causing my eyes to slowly close

As my bare feet play—in the coolness of the stream
Where the fawn slowly drinks
From the nape of my neck
Tickle does the flow of water about my feet

Now I feel the softness of the wind
Grazing my eyelashes as if to say
I'll be back this way
Oh how this breeze soaks me with kisses
Without the use of lips
Finding that hollow place—in the nape of my neck

The robin becomes weary
After it's long journey
Seeking shelter and a place to rest—for the night
She tucks her soft feathers against my face—then
Gently nudges her way into the nape of my neck

Baby gazelles are summoned to dance
By the music found in my ear
Precious is the sound
Acknowledges the opening of my eyes
Only to find that you my love
Asleep in my dream

For you washed my feet, kissed me slowly and whispered
    softly to me
Becoming dreamy you cuddle next to me
The quietness of your hair rests against my skin

I'm awaken by the tender rhythm of your breathing
From the gentle movement of your breasts
I exert little effort in my gaze upon you
Though I feel so much love as I take you back to my
    dream
Holding you close as we fill that hollow spot
Carved in the nape of my neck

Chocolate Date

Your chocolate handprint—on my white shirt
Isn't all I have to take with me after our date
Your childlike laughter still lingers in the back of my
   mind
While I continue to try and remember where did you
Get the chocolate from

Now on my bed alone I replay each word you said
Rewinding the way your eyes sparkled when you smiled
The placement of your fingers when you held my hand
Fast forwarding to my emotions within—
Pausing on how this night with you makes me feel—
My memory records the beauty of our date
Did I erase the chocolate scene?

I sleep anxiously because of the thoughts
Of what fun we might have tomorrow
My smile caresses my heart as if to say
My thoughts of you are just as special as you are to me
So I close my eyes holding tightly to our blissful kiss
   goodnight

Still I'm wondering—when did you have chocolate?
Or am I so taken by our date and all that it offered
That your chocolate handprint on my white shirt
Is enough of a mystery about love for me until our next
   date

Waterless Tears

Waterless tears
Invite me to run to the water
That shall bathe me
Washing me

The ears of my heart
Tingle at the sound
Of water dripping in my spirit
Crying to my soul

Soaked am I
By waterless tears
Which minister to the river
Made by voiceless rain

Cleanse me
Is my request
My painful utterance—resting upon
Shoulders of tears in the past

My sun licked face
Is the creator of this desert
Longing for the clouds to open
Relieving the storm within

My joy is silent in the stillness
Oh the aroma of peace
May the flood of forgiveness overtake me
May the water of time baptize me
Having mercy on my cry and my waterless tears

Sometimes

Sometimes nothing is so complicated
Than that of a simple thought

Sometimes nothing is so painful
Than that when pleasure is sought

Sometimes nothing is so awful
Than that of a kind word

When praises are received
Yet praise is none deserved

Sometimes nothing is so honest
Than that of the unknown truth

Sometimes nothing is so beyond years
Than that of an old youth

Sometimes nothing is so childlike
Than that of a childless past

Sometimes nothing moves so slow
Than he who dies so fast

So when you feel you have nothing
I ask that you look again

Because sometimes nothing can be a lot better
Than having something that's worth nothing

My Trouble — My Father

People often ask why I act the way I do
Sit down my brother—let me explain to you
You see my father wasn't around
And with my mother always gone
Trouble is what I found
For with him I'm never alone
No particular direction—do we ever take
My trouble—my father, is your first mistake
Any crime you can think of
Yes we have done
Not out of hate nor love—not even just for fun
For reasons I can never explain
When attempting to do so, I tend to feel the pain
If mother had been home—or at least less of a friend
And father I guess—well if you would have just been

Timeless Dream

If I choose to believe
Therefore it must be
That I could make you—a dream
My reality

If my vision is blurred
By emotions alone
Do I not dare reach
For that which I long

But if in my quest—I should fail
To seek that which is mine
I would have gained the greatest gift
That gift being your time

Make My Bed

The smile of this love
Gives me power to place my hand through stone
And on the other side make my bed the bosom of joy
Where I sleep with my ear to the east of her heart

This love finds me with outstretched hands
To the quail in the cleft of the rock
Offering all that I am
To a love that makes a nest in my heart

Oh how the berries grow in the garden of fragrance
I feed on my affection for you until day turns night
Through my pores love seeps
Making sweet wine for your lips to taste

My unattended soul is incomplete without her
Lovely are her eyes, which marry the eyes of my heart
I forgive the eloping of my spirit
When her lovely voice called me by name

My love how beautiful you are
All of life's gentlemen grow fond of you
Though it is I who shall take delight
In my find of such tender fruit

On this day she completes me
Pouring into me like water
Invading all chambers of my being
Easing ache of thirst, birthing new and old life

Tonight I sleep in the bosom of this love
Knowing that with every breath we take
We consummate this love like branches on a tree
Which suddenly bloom with flowers
Because it is love—I love you so much

I Ain't Got

I ain't got nobody
No I ain't got no one
I ain't got no money
And I ain't got no fun
I had cheer and laughter
Money and a lot of joy
But you took all of that
When you walked out the door
I'm not one to give up
I just stand aside
But you took my spirit
And a little of my pride
Although you took almost everything
You were considerate to leave behind
A whole lot of tears
And this broken heart of mine
I hope you're doing just fine
But I thought you should know
That I ain't got nobody
Every since you decided to go
I ain't got nobody
No—I ain't got no one
I ain't got no money
And I ain't got no fun

More Time

I have an engagement with the present
This passionate moment holds my devotion
I kiss the hourglass
Which pains tomorrow to give me more time
My soul collides with unwritten thoughts
Sparks of dumbfounded knowledge comes to life
Paining my past as it asks for more time

I have an engagement with the present
A golden candle is lit
Representing verbal love and the seduction of
    conversation
Welcoming my past and future
To operate simultaneously
As I romance the gentleness of breath
Which caresses the present, which has no more time

Much Love

Much love to my brother
He who has no mother to care
Much love to my brother
He's dying without a prayer
Much love to my brother
With no more tears to cry
Much love to my brother
And his "god," which is getting high
Much love to my brother
Even if his thoughts are not like my own
Much love to my brother
When he judges me by my skin tone
Much love to my brother
As he hates me both day and night
Much love to my brother
At the moment he decides to take my life
Much love to my brother
Going through life without a plan
Much love to my brother
With my blood on his hands
And as I lie dying
From hate's bullet to the head
Much love to my brother
Yes—he who wished me dead

Signals

Are there any signs?
Before you leave this earth
Signals often given
Yet we overlook their worth
Is there a great deed we will do?
Because we have never done one before
Or is the thought of death last week
Yet we simply ignored
Is the feeling that today
Is different than the others
Or was it the pain you had last night
When you knew you missed your mother
Could it be the voice you hear
When no one's around
Or could it be the eyes on you
With no face to be found
Is death giving signals?
Be warned if you might
For death in an instance
Will take us like a thief in the night

Resurrected Voice

As the sun warms my face from the clouds it peeps
    through
From this moment—this time—I'm reminded of you
Even though my eyes don't see you everyday
My mind does realize you're just a thought away
Your smile so bright and heart so true
Makes one search the reason for the answer—why you
I wipe another tear from my tear stained face
My heart filled with pain and anger yet there's an empty
    space
Where love once occupied—oh I remember such joy
I fear I'll never love again—as I did before
Forgive me if I try—I ask—I pray
For blessed is he who turns to the Lord they say
My soul feels beaten by the lashes of death's whip
Body so weak, makes me question am I not equipped
To deal with such hurt—with pain so deep
I acknowledge that I'm not—I do so cowardly
So many voices in my head—some yell while others
    scream
A voice did whisper "remember me," it seems
Quickly I move—to find a place—where I might feel safe
Now my eyes start the search
For the voice without a face

Hu — Man

A man who lives
Is a man who dies
A man who talks
Is a man who lies
A man who gives
Is a man who takes
A man who loves
Is a man who hates
A man who can
Is a man who won't
And men who do
Are men who don't
For a man is
But only a man
He's nothing more—nothing less
Than A Man

A Moment

Listen to the soft wind as it blows
Watch the rushing water as it flows
Hug the sunrays as it heats
Feel your heart as it beats
Seek the love from within thyself
Then spread that love to someone else

Act 1 Scene 2

Do I dare indulge in my loving passion for you?
I invite not this wrath
The darkness of the most hidden
Private shadows need no sun
My mind not being depraved
Tends to make me worthy of life
Tragic would it be to ponder lust
To simply be turned over to it
As though separated from wrong and right
This created and mystical passion however small
Has shone itself greater than my strength to hide it
Asking me to exchange what is real to me
For that which is unbeknownst to you
This existence of passion I have for you
Leaves me wounded and weak
Therefore my healing lies in my ability to forgive
An indulgence that slithers shamefully within me

My Due Season

She is my due season
She is the remaining of same things changed
She is perfection wanting for nothing
She is this beautiful moment
Presented to time as a gift
She is my due season
Causing my whole life to change
I adore her beauty
I sink into the softness of it
For she falls on me like winter
Frozen do I become—at such raw beauty
And like the season of spring
I became a new-as she smiled and walked away
Her beauty completes my summer
Making her my due season

The Stolen Kiss

Darkness is made to be my lady
She whispers, "You are not alone"
In the ear which has not found her lips
Oh but her touch against my trembling body
Covers the nakedness of my open soul
The roaring of my heart does not frighten her

Darkness is made to be my lady
For her I crucify my flesh
Sacrificing its will to control my desire
My feelings for her grow like wild strawberries
My eyes attempt to go to her
As if sight would reveal to me such beauty

Darkness is made to be my lady
And she holds me tenderly—and I love her more
Her love is greater than most things I've ever known
In my mind, my hands create her lips so that I might be
    kissed
Sadness smiles at my longing to love her more than before
As dawn taps my shoulder while it kisses my lady "Hello"

Posture

Though I sleep with barely closed eyes
I call to you
Tonight I attempt to banish—a fresh frenzy of memories
Because my insatiable desire has an intense craving to seek
    the face of love
Now awaken by embedded disheveled secrets and dreams
Which are half dressed in the quietness of disturbed
    moments
I search the night air in hopes that it would provide words
Or even give language to the reasons I love you so

In my dreams, you alone
Like a single petal lost in the wilderness of my thoughts
Take steps towards me imitating the falling of leaves
At times you seek to find your way out
At times you tend to make my words your home
And there we live
In yet to be articulated feelings

Then soon I'm lured to the edge of her river
To stand at the bank of her boundless grace
With sleep breathing gently on me—time becomes
    confusing
Then I, like over ripened fruit, which falls from the tree
    branch
I kneel at the footstool of the one I love
Realizing as I lay to sleep
That a love such as this
Can buckle my knees regardless of my posture

Land Of Dreams

I've awaken from the land of dreams
Where the bitterness of winter
Uses frozen breath and the stillness thereof
To beckon the liveliness of spring to come forth
Articulate is the greenery
As its lushes lips smiles upon the earth
I'm charmed by the giant trees and their persuasive limbs
Which carefully blindfold my love for the sun
I journey into the forest—down into a place called Crying
    Valley
Here I hope to discover all that I've ever lost
My steps are deep but not careful—painfully I've placed
    my feet
Into a decently laid trap of my memory
For my thoughts of you touch me deeply
Deeper than the marrow of bone—without compassion it
    will not let me go
High above doves fly and coo as if knowing my sorrow
My journey continues with the light of the sun
A deer crosses my path with her provocative rhythmic
    steps
Suddenly she stops and looks into my eyes
Burying her heart into my spirit—as if she wished to heal
My unfulfilled desire to love and my untraceable trail of
    lost
The doves tug at my feet and guide my heart
To a pond in Crying Valley so that I might wait on the
    new moon
My reflection in the water has closed its eyes
To distort the memories of lost love

The water muffles the love secrets—hidden under tear
    stained rocks
So here this night I will sleep—leaving love and lost
    awake
To continue the journey in Crying Valley—
Only to stop and rest in my land of dreams

III.. Uninvited Feelings

Uninvited Feelings

I held your hands searching for your heart
For the moment is mine for the taking
Uninvited feelings you stirred in me
This love could never be shaken
I'm born again looking into your eyes
My spirit a runaway being
Eternally grateful—to the heavens—I would be
If your heart would beat—to that which I'm seeking

Untraceable Love

The fear to love blinds me
Causing my nerves to heighten
I become more aware
Of the passion which frightens me

If I'm to face my fear
Then I must surrender myself
To the forbidden fire—
To that which has driven sensible me insane

My eyes are of no use to me
For it is my heart that shall be my guide
Uncovering this mystery
Which hides behind confusion masking my pain

Oh how I long to love
I wish to be in love
That need to feel loved

Yet, I would never be happy with that part of myself
Because then I'm at the mercy of trust

For some it's the destroyer of lives
For me—it is the blindfold placed softly over my eyes

A Reservoir of Affection

Soothing and Beautiful is the consistency of love
Oh the logic of it all
Simply conjures up a thirst that only the liquid
From love's breast is fruit enough to hold me hostage
Making me incapable of speech
As if I would want to utter a sound
While delighting myself with every sensuous taste
My mouth dare not set free provocative dreams
Therefore bringing forth pain
Because I would want to dream again
So that I might drink once more
From the breast that nurtures
Allowing me to find intimacy
In the sweet nectar found in love's breast
For there I've found consistency for love
In love's reservoir of affection

Embracing Tenderness
(A Rose)

The softness of the rose
Which embraces me so tenderly
Feels though I might die from it

The petal swells with ripe color
Until it's beauty spills over
Bursting through frozen veins

My hand and the rose dance
To a melody
Sound cannot comprehend

Suddenly I'm pierced by a thorn
The sharpness of pain
Causes separation of music and love

Brought forth by the betrayal
Of the sensuous beauty of a rose
Making anguish's fragrance

A scent of a poetic love affair
Making the pure pleasure of the rose
Tenderness appreciated and embraced by the eye from
    afar

Starving For Your Love

I'm craving you, my love
My desire has a hunger
As if just traveled the birth canal
Eager to show an awaiting passion
Thus the reason I was born
Oh my love,
Fluttering are my feelings-
Like white tipped feathers in a soft breeze
Kissing my urging silence to speak
Which whispers, "Let me taste the sweet dripping
     affections of your love"
For my ravishing appetite is unfulfilled
Impatient I grow
Ungratifying is the unconquered grace
Which pours from her lips
So I delight myself in a dream of an acquired desire
Your beauty though haunts my dream
While I eagerly await the slumber of sleep
Under the watchful eye of the stars
Starving for your love

Sea To Sand

I lend my voice to the merging of sea to sand
So that this day might harbor the existence of love
Duplicated is the sound of the wind
which forbids the softness of angelic wings from above
to float across the sky, ride upon a breeze
And to force the right now of things already happened

My heart openly declares my love for you
My words I can no longer swallow—as grains of sand
they fall upon the earth
The sea washes about my feet—to gorge itself on the
    honey
that drips from my tongue
So that it might carry such sweet passion back from
    whence it came

My whole heart is imprinted in the sand where I stand
My love for you saturates me—
And as the sea takes from the sand—is my love gratefully
    given
without anything expected in return
Quivering is my voice, which questions—
How does my soul dare stay dry from love waters, which
    flood over me?

As my love for you lends itself to the merging of sea to
    sand

Enhanced Appreciation

Again I awake
With the sun upon my face
Another day I'm blessed
So I welcome morning's embrace

I listen to the birds chirp
They seem so nearby
I hear the flapping of the mother's wings
As she takes off to fly

I feel the coolness of air
As it brushes across my skin
A touch so soft
I'm overjoyed from within

I hear laughter of children
Preparing to go play
Indeed I'm blessed
Is what I must say

A delight to smell the earth
The rich soil far beneath
Another taste of morning
And it is oh so sweet

And yes, I pray this morning
As I did so last night
I'm blessed to see another day
Even though I have no sight

My World Of Her

Her smile is like the sun
As it captures and warms my heart
Her voice soft as a breeze
Like the dew
as the day does start

Dark are her eyes, which glisten
With a touch of starry innocence
The birds make a cheerful sound
As if to gain her acceptance

Hello world
It seems she states
It is she the world tends to acknowledge
Witnessed by a smile of rainbow shape
And creatures' dance of jolly

A wonderful creation she is
This woman
This lovely sight
Heaven and earth smile all day
Then lovingly watched her sleep by night

It is love that has been written
Yes written upon my very soul
This day my heart's voice is honored
For—her beauty
My world's eye beholds

Thou Remnant Prayer

Dear Lord in heaven and of all the earth
As a sinner I speak for what it's worth
On bended knees and with head in hand
Your forgiveness I seek but would understand
If my breath would be taken as I speak
My heart became heavy to never again beat
Please give me this moment—this space in time
To pray for peace and a better mankind
What right do I have to ask for such things?
From the Lord of Lords and the King of Kings
Well as a sinner I know and have come to learn
That through out man's journey he constantly yearns
For a greater love—much greater than himself
Such as power from conquering or the abundance of
      wealth
Fools of LIFE'S game—yes—we have become
But no longer will I play—for I seek your Kingdom
So forgive us Lord—for we know not what we do
Have mercy on our souls
As you show us the greatest love is you

Secret Twinkle

When I wish upon the stars
I look into your eyes
That's where the secrets of the twinkle
Are examined never criticized

As my heart pounds like a drum
The heavens open wide
The rivers overflow
When I look into your eyes

I'm a lost soul that's been found
A spirit that has no shame
I'm a candle that's long burned out
But your eyes have lit a flame

A beauty that glows day and night
As captured sparkles in my mind
The tenderness of loving eyes
Is what my eyes have longed to find

This secret an uninvited feeling
Yet it has now arrived
For the twinkle of the stars
Have been found within your eyes

Intolerable Pleasure

Today I feel as though I've been denied air
My heart is heavy—I swallow deeply
As though I could truly digest my hurt
The pain from this fresh wound
Makes me dizzy
For I'm all that's left of our parted love
In and out of consciousness are my emotions
Slowly I'm drifting to a place of disbelief
My mind tends not to lose the memories
Of a once known pleasure
Forgetting seems to forever stay
My thoughts confirming why my heart cries
Therefore making real this torturous moment
Tender was the love I bestowed upon you
This love shared exhorted our souls
Now intolerable is this once known pleasure
As I take the last sweet breaths
Of a parted love and all that it has left

Opinionated Love

Love to me is protecting
That which I call my own
Love to me is hating
That which is unknown
Love to me is keeping
Everything for myself
Love to me is never
Respecting anything or anyone else

To Me It Seems

To me it seems
Her lips make sweet my stolen kiss
As she takes from the moon, and gives to me the sun
I swim in her sky
While my love is cloaked in the perfection of a teardrop
Like mist I fall—
Floating towards everything—stopping at nothing
Then in secret it seems she pours into my ear
The fruit of words—"You cannot steal that which has
    been tenderly given"
So I take her hands in mine
And we walk upon the stars
Warm is my sun making diamonds out of tears
Which slowly fade with the coming of a new day
Because of her my world seems pure
And under the eyes of heaven we kiss
With her love sealed in my heart
With my love embraced in her arms

Patiently I Wait

My touch to yours
Your touch to mine
Creating a force so powerful
A bond so sensitive
I seem not to have the strength to hide
The awakening of my senses
My desire to taste you
My want to see you
My need to hear and smell you
My hope to hold you
I yearn for understanding
I long for the explanation
Patiently I wait

The Weeping Of My Heart

My heart cried for you last night
My eyes shed not a tear
My mouth spoke not a word
But my body asked for you here

My mind keeps happy thoughts
The past memories of days so bright
My ears hunger for your sweet laughter
But no sound fills my appetite

My heart cried for you last night
And of this I'm not ashamed
For the ache in my soul is forever deep
Caused by seeking pleasure from pain

So if you're touched by raindrops
Ever so softly in the face
It's just my unhidden tears
For your love I can't replace

Although I hope to love another
And pray somehow from you depart
Just know I'll still be wiping tears
Even if it is the weeping of my heart

Fear Glows In The Dark

This flower only blooms at night
For "fear" of the daylight
Opening up for all to see
To be accepted—yet—that's not to be

Awakening to the night's embrace
With the sense of insecurity erased
My flower glows ever so bright
For darkness has become the flower's light

Your Bouquet

Your hair is like a bouquet of flowers
Using alluring colors to try and clothe its naked beauty
The smell of your hair spewing gloriously into the air
This delicate love scent is everywhere yet very hard to find
A garden of worship is your hair
Where doves hide only to be found by intrusive eyes
How diluted am I to think
I could indulge myself in your bed of cluster
By such beauty one can easily be betrayed
Each strand woven together to form
An art of painting that gingerly caresses
The eye of the beholder
Whose fingers, which long to touch
Your bouquet of flowers

If We Are

We are the people that make the world
We are the colors that make the swirl
We are the millions that make this one
Where evil versus good up and under the sun

Our eyes cried once many tears
We are the blood shed for so many years
With a merciful God looking from the sky
We are the minds that wonder why
If love and hate share our hearts
Why are we the people tearing our brothers apart?

Embraced Absent Hands

This night you've touched my heart
Absent Hands
Plunging your tongue
Deep into my spongy mind
Aching is the arching of my neck
As it holds the net—attempting to trap emotions
Which jump about my soul like fish out of water
Air tends to hide from me

Such beauty makes flesh of all that language is
Embracing tightly my thoughts
Absent Hands
Oh that the moon be born twice this night
Granting my eyes the fortune to
Look upon your beauty and reflect why my love knows
    no sleep
Permitting my ears to cherish your every word
As I balance myself upon your parted lips

This night you've touched my heart
Absent Hands
My wish is to drink from your cup of beauty
To have the palms of my hands grasp this adorable taste
And swallow
Romantically intoxicated I would become
Enough so that I would hand over my heart
So that your heart might embrace me
Absent Hands
Making present this night your touch
No longer absent
Embracing my heart

My Painted Vision

They say their mother is baking
And their father, he's at work
Every Sunday they dress up and attend this building they
    call a church

But where I live—I smell only the dampness of the air
And to mother and father I'd say I love you
If I thought they really would care
Young as I may be—my goals are very clear
My painted picture of where I'm from
Is to get away from here

My mother sometimes hits me
Because my father is never around
My ache is not from hurt
But for love which isn't found
I draw strength from where I am, because this is all I know
My vision will be my brush, to paint the picture
Of where I'll go

The Perspective Of My Soul

I put the ownership to love you on me
I put the responsibility to love you on me
To be in love with you
Where else would the responsibility be?

The frighten part of me accepts being in love with you
Should I though allow that part of me to make such a
    decision?

The gift you offer to me
Which is to love
Such a worthy treasure
It's more than the eyes can see
More than the heart can feel

Connecting with you has allowed me to become closer to
    me
For I've used this circumstance as an opportunity to grow

Do I have the right to love you and if so shouldn't I
    choose to exercise it
You are the perspective of my soul
I indulge and simply wallow in the depth of this love
This experience so intense
Making my heart acknowledge the excruciating pleasure
Recognizing my desire to love you
Accepting the responsibility of my choice

And if love is not returned to me
It is I—at the end of the day
Who is held accountable for my decision to love?

The Conclusion Of Beauty

I'm envious of that which I have no understanding
My ignorance clothes my nakedness
Which comes from the lack of knowledge
The lack of knowledge of my mind's attempt to interpret
The vision my eyes have seen
Which is your indescribable beauty
Appearing before the world
Sharing every secret—granting me permission
To admire that which only time would want to steal
Your beauty touches me
As no hand I've ever felt
It moves me like no words ever spoken
To truly love you would be a feat near impossible
Though the want to love you completes my being
Your beauty ask nothing of me
Yet it gives to me it's all
My desire to understand is consuming
Thus I've come to this conclusion
Your beauty is both cruel and kind
Cruel because it refuses to go away
Kind because it accepts me as I am

Lady, Rose

This rose is for you
For the lady you are
This petal represents your eyes
My shining stars
This petal represents your smile
That restores my confidence
This petal represents your touch
That assures my existence
This petal represents your thoughts
That comprehends my being
This petal represents your beauty
That gives love a new meaning
This petal represents your heart
So loving and so kind
The stem belongs to me
Because I'm so glad you are mine

Innocence

How I often wonder
Do children really understand?
The things that happen around them
The good, the evil, the sad
"Mommy taught me well," said one
As he smiled a candid smile
"Mommy has closed her eyes," he said
Now she's going to sleep for a while
I've been waiting on mommy
To wake up from her long sleep
She promised to bake some cookies
Then come outside and play with me
Daddy said he was off to work
But he's not home from his job
He told mommy goodbye so nicely
It really made her sob
The child began to play in the dirt
He was the innocent, the free, the new
"I'll be glad when mommy wakes up," he said
"Cause we have a lot to do"

I Wanted To Thank You

Because of you I know that my birth was not a mistake
My existence on earth is warranted
Because of you it is fate
For I've found in you
What others search a lifetime for
My appreciation for this blessing
Is known by the angels
The clapping of their hands is as loud as a lion's roar
I want to take this moment to thank you
I thank you for loving me
And for giving me the courage to open my heart
Allowing my encounter with love to have no boundaries
Your smile brightens the sky—
Your love is a must
It reminds me of a gentle kiss
Which causes the sun to blush

Attempt

The power of the weak
Is so very strong
The world stands and watches
Its eyes open wide
A smile upon its face
As the weak searches to realize
That our fear is the strength
Yet we deny it because of doubt
Quietly you weep
Let the world hear you shout
Can not's will become I can
Or at least let me try
Before the attempt—a prayer
Lord please don't let me die
So afraid not to succeed
What would the story tell?
Not trying leaves no question
The answer—you've already failed
Hear me—to the small—to the poor
The too sad to even seek
Attempting could be the power
That makes the world take a seat

Un-Languaged Love

Compelled am I to speak honestly
Of my true love for you
Desperately do I love
Sacred are the moments, which somehow become a new

I crawl in the belly of the earth
Searching for the root from which your love stems
Hoping to gather the fruit of joy in which love bares
Tasteful is the strength provided from the pulp of a love
    not condemned

I search for love through the hate and the wrong
I hum the sound of love's music
Because I do not know the words to its song

I want my fingers to feel the words of which you speak
Attempting to trace the steps of your love
Intimately guide me my love
As my heart listens to night following the sun above

I painfully conceal my love from you
Yet my soul is marked each time we meet
Your presence kisses my lonely spirit
To deserve your love is what I seek

This one life of love I give willingly
My sacred cry is for the life of two
For there is no mortal love ever greater
Than the unlanguaged love I have for you

Consumption

I want to savor the splendor of love
Have my body taste and my mind consume
All that love has to give
Rejecting nothing
Let the journey of my fingertips
Trace the contours of love's face
So that I might reveal the mystery
Covering this delicacy
My mouth travels the familiar river path
Reaching the peak of the mountains
Gentle is the air that speaks to my ear
As if urging the continuation of my tongue
Which seeks the delicious pleasures
Of sensations I cannot yet account for
Tiny eruptions are felt as if they were
The rising and falling of waves
My hunger is tossed
My eyes though detect the ripening of love's fruit
It's juices soliciting to come forth
My lips welcome each drop
I absorb the aroma while I tightly embrace my smiling
    palate
Now once again I want to savor the splendor of love
So that I may taste all that love has to give

Sleeping In My Dream

Sweet is my sleep when I dream of her
Precious is she—
Like rubies and gold

Retained in my heart is my love for her
Desiring the day it is she I hold

I sleep in the loneliness of a rocking chair
With each movement
I dance with flirtation

Timeless is her untouched beauty
Elegant the music of meditation

She has become my rose
My dream her vase
Delicately is she placed

Luscious are her petals
Which dangle like grapes
Full of bloom bursting with taste

I adore you like Christmas
In the month of July
Joyfully close yet so far

A dream distant away
Reminding my sleep
In my heart we are never apart

The Shape Of Flesh

From here the cleavage of apple halves
Welcomes the warmth of my stare
While my hands guide my eyes down the pathway of
    faraway love
While my eyes navigate my hands over golden
    flesh—toward glistening seeds
How special I feel as two-apple halves offer me the delight
    of wholeness
Pure and fresh is the apple's bosom
Who told you about my love for your sun ripened skin
My love for your apple halves, which lay before me
    smooth and naked
Like two countries sharing the same land
Let me invade each country—uncovering the summer
Untangling the vines
Let me search each corner of their roundness
Allow me to hunt under their rivers
I will use my tongue to carve my name into the soft naked
    land
Announcing my arrival—claiming the apples halves and
    its cleavage
Conquering the yearn to be explored
The apple's beautiful bosom shadows all—
Covering the arrangements of this moment
Which is formed by the shape of flesh
Yes, how special to me is the tenderness of their posture
That I've become a connoisseur of the cleavage of apple
    halves
For perfection is each half—with its own identity
My mouth simply savors the texture of golden flesh
My fingers give honor to the glistening seeds

When night approaches and calls me to sleep
I cover each apple half with a kiss
Therefore making my apple whole
Realizing that from the core will emerge love and beauty

No Place To Go

What must I do with these feelings?
These feelings that tend to love you so
I've asked that they leave me
They tell me they have no place to go

I told the universe the story
Of how you took my heart
And how the stolen gift
Is only missed when we're apart

What must I do with this love?
This love that loves you so
I understand why love can't leave me
Because without you- my love has no place to go

IV.. Another Conversation

You've Not Yet Left

You've not yet left
But your presence I already miss
Like the autumn breeze against the leaves
Trembling are my feelings within

The coldness of the night grips my hand
Stealing the warmth of our last touch
Aware of how I miss you so
Absent the fact you stand before me

If ever one was made for another
It is you and I
Like fire we have burned into the other's life
And my love becomes a flame all over again
Every time I see you

Forever is what I see in your eyes
Echoing long after our embrace goodnight
The moonlight makes day of night
As I watch your silhouette walk slowly away

The crickets chirped a happy song
And I promise I saw the owl smile
When you turn back to hug me once more

Acoustically does my heart sing
As I hold you tight
Expressing my joy

You've not yet left
But your presence I miss
As we say goodnight—at your front door

Johnny Creeps

In the deepest of the night
When all seems asleep
For evil isn't still
For my friend Johnny Creeps
From the North to the East
He lurks in the dark
Johnny creeps in the nighttime
But in the day he departs
So at night if you feel eyes watching
But the eyes are not there
It's just Johnny Creeps
So stop and take care

Dark Of My Dreams

I close my eyes to search for you
Because if I believe—
Then dreams do come true

You are as far as I hope and as close as I wish
As I'm guided by a light your beauty has kissed

My mind has created a person that my heart wants to
    trust
In darkness your love shines—
Hidden not—
To me your love is a must

Love's Captive

I've punished my soul
By letting my heart feel for you
The moment I started to care
I became a prisoner
Held in captivity by an emotion
Do I dare disturb or better yet anger
That which I do not understand
I pause for a moment
I hear the silence
To me it screams so loud
My tears answer the confusion, which confines me
While in my captivity—I thank you
For allowing me to be me
In doing so she—being you—takes my breath
For the words which lay softly upon my lips
Feel heavy on the tongue as I try to speak
The emotion of love and not the act of love consumes me
Loose me I pray—my prayer goes unanswered
How long must I want for you?
The mere thought I would ever need you
Violates my core being forever—daring to love another
In this setting the mystery of love is my tormenter
For it has my mind and heart chained and bounded
Free me I beg of you
Help me someone to escape the desire to love
And forever I would be in your debt
This love has no sense of time
So I'm hoping I'll become stronger
Because in this moment—I punish my soul
By telling my heart I feel for you no longer

My Prayer's Prayer

I write this realizing
You find no substance in my words
I guess my prayer's prayer is that
When you are able to trust again
You would find me there
Now I may never be the reason
You would dare open your heart to trust
But hope you would allow me to help
Nurture your faith in miracles
My heart certainly treasures
The gifts you've provided me—things such as
An opportunity to laugh out loud
The moment to find not a star in the sky
Yet I'm always able to find small twinkles in your eyes
A kiss on the cheek
The chance to have sharing conversation and to spend
    precious hours
Which seem like gentle seconds with you
For this I realize
That heaven must have a heart
And for these things—I say thank you
I'm sadly aware that the earning of trust
Is an expense that spares not the heart, mind nor soul
But it is a price that I'm willing to bear

The Sealed Treasure

In my heart lies the greatest treasure
Ever known to man
It shines brighter than a diamond
For it is the love of a woman

Real love is priceless and weighs more than
Any amount of gold
Unspoken words are heard
The look in her eyes—rich men hope to hold

The trust of her touch is genuine
No money could feel so real
I will protect the value of her love
With my life—for my heart has placed love's seal

A Decision

I heard my heart yet obeyed my mind
I felt the years without keeping time
I've wished upon stars and prayed to beliefs
My life now taken how do I rest in peace?

My Silence

My silence is often times confused
With my willingness to participate or to share
That though is so far from the truth
I've come to understand that in my attempt to learn
I must first acknowledge the presence of God
In my acknowledgement my spirit is quiet
So that my meditation is not disturbed or interrupted
I've found laying this peaceful foundation
Enhances my ears to hear the spoken word
And allows my heart to seek the unspoken message

Faith — (Innocence Of Hands)

The sunless days
Evokes teasing of my sophisticated tongue
Making brilliant the place
Where sunshine is invited
A place where articulate thoughts
Are visions of soon to come future
Inviting the hands of innocence
To put their trust in a prayer
Which might give existence to hopelessness
Vindicating all who seek to inquire
In a faith more forgiving than that of their own
Allowing mercy to be offered
And praises to be spoken
For desires yet unseen by the eye
For the tongue is often only
A representation of the heart's beliefs

Your Heart I Hope Accepts

I apologize for the things I said
Also for the things I've done
I apologize to you my dear
For hurting you is no fun

I apologize to you this way
So you would know my actions are true
Is an apology in the beauty of a rose?
No my dear—no beauty matches you

With words I say I'm sorry
A rose can't represent the depth
Your smile would mean you heard me
But it's your heart I hope accepts

Taste, Wind & Thorns

The regurgitation of my thoughts
Is rich in nourishment and is adorable in taste
In comparison to the milk contained in a mother's breast
A constant reminder that my needs lie
In a want to find a fresh unprejudiced thought
So that my mouth is not tempted to speak the bitterness
Which remains on the tongue of my heart

I've come to realize the silence between us has died
Now empty is my day
I find myself lately reaching for the wind
As if to hold it in my hands
So that I might make use of it—
To use it as water
So that I may wash away all residue of hurtful thoughts

Wrinkled are the anguish clothes of the wind
Making it impossible for my hands to hold
Slow is the pain, which curves around my thoughts
Hunting about my soul as though for prey
Testing my endurance while invading my rest
And the wind knows not my touch
Therefore it knows not my thoughts

Immaculate she stands before me
In my dreams—in my sleepless dreams
Yes the dreams I soak in prayer
The love inside of me has once again awakened
Then the thorn of a thought pierces me deeply
Reminding me discolored are my feelings
Towards a love that would bloom a thought
Regardless of the bitter plant of pain
Regardless of a love that would leave a taste of
    unforgetfulness

Beauty Is Her Heart

Beauty she is that's all she knows
She presents it to the world wherever she goes
Her confidence in self and with a smile that glows
Reflecting beauty she is for that's all she knows
Intelligent lady- no mistake in design
Nothing more beautiful than the beauty of her mind
With her voice so soft—gentle as a breeze
Her words are liquid, which quenches my thirst
Placing an aching soul at ease
Her eyes are like windows—open for all to see
There's beauty in her spiritual vision—one day we all
    must seek
Tender moments she offers—
For her beauty is the spark
I present to you an unwrapped gift
The beauty of her heart

His Story Of Her Smile

A moment unforgotten
Time seems unforgiving
The heart does keep forever records
As I celebrate the knowing of her smile
A smile, which has shown me its nakedness
While dressing me in its warmth
After bathing me in timeless memories
How my heart feels the sound of her eyes saying hello
Softly wrapping her smile's ancient embrace
Around me—suspending time
Carrying me down a path I've traveled before
Making familiar all that is good

Occasions such as this, time hopes to steal, make rusty
Yet her smile protects my heart and polishes my soul
Clothe am I for any season
Let me give back to her all that she has bestowed upon me
Antique has been her gift
Eternity documents this historic moment
Her smile—I share
Yet never departing from it

The Vault Of My Mind

My experiences should be
Could be
The inscribable novels lost within
The vault of my mind
Embellished syllables
Unpronounceable letters
Making lines of non-useful words
Across an unforgiving page
Making fiction stories unacceptable
Therefore gorgeous imaginary thoughts
Flow off the watery tongue and spill unto the paper
Smearing the language of my untold fables
Chapter after chapter penetrating the eyes
Touching the heart
While the life inside of me cries
Given existence to uncaptured feelings
Because they wallow in the depth of my silence

Picture Of A Castle

I can't get you out of my head
Your love has reached the depth of my soul
My heart has painted a bloody picture
But every stroke your beauty did control

I can't get you out of my head
Maybe I'm not as strong as I claim to be
Love and joy you've tampered with
Body and soul you've made weak

I can't get you out of my head
A palace I've built for you in my mind
A tear for that bloody castle
That bleeds time after time

The Eyes' Touch Of Pleasure

Perfect harmony—is my touch
Upon your skin
Causing my heart to beat faster
Every time my eyes reach for you
As I hope to touch and discover
Places that are unknown—but yet found within you
Intrusive is the pleasure to my soul
Craving rest from the travels of indulgence
Though welcoming the offer of eternal bliss
Oh the touch of voiceless love
And how my eyes absorb your velvet flesh
Stroking the melodious passion
Found within your eyes
Soothing the heart's chorus of transparent emotion
Perfect harmony is my gaze
Into your eyes
Creating a song only heard
Every time our eyes find each other
Placing lyrics in my heart
Which says I'll be loving you forever

A Painted Picture

They say the grass is green
The sky is always blue
And people often say hello, and ask how are you
But where I live I'm blind—to colors that others seem to
    see
And deaf to people speaking in voices filled with peace
For my grass is stained with blood
Which makes for a rusty look
And my sky is often gray
Sometimes blue with mental input
My neighbors are the strangers
When we are in the street
No words ever exchange and our eyes never meet
But the silence is always broken
With screams and sounds of guns
This is my painted picture
Of the world where I'm from

The Palace Song
(King)

May my words be precious to your eyes
May your ears be attentive to my voice
May heaven open up
As I confess my love to you
May my tongue bless your name
As often as it pours from my lips
May mercy find me forever
Giving strength to an unclothed prayer
For naked and open I stand before thee
And I confess my wicked ways
May the repenting of my sins
Cleanse my soul—make my heart joyful
And lengthen my precious days

Written Upon The Heart

For love to be then I must perceive it to be
I've embraced the thought of not feeling
I've accepted never to be known by love
For you've emptied me of love
And you stayed not to fill me back up
Now there is a hole where my heart should be
Through your eyes I searched for your heart
But how can I ever have faith in a love I can't see

The intimacy of love could never equal this intimacy of
    pain
I realize something wonderful was stolen when I lost you
Yet was love taken from me or did I relinquish it
Must I put myself in a place of surrender?
The bitterness of an unknown love
Is a blessing in my life
Which has descended upon me
As a message on an angel's wing
Written upon my heart

A Melody

Love does not have to speak its name
For me to know that it exist
Faraway silence makes distance close
As skin shouts
Shouts so that my heart may hear a voice that attempts to
    fade
Into the wind when love speaks its name

I've come to this place of love
Yet love has not come to me
I stand still in my confusion
The moon shines in my heart
Illuminating all of love's nonexistence
Broken am I in my lost

I submerge myself in her love
Knowing she loves me
I fear not drowning
As love introduces me once again to the being within
A ripe sweet future accepts the gift of love's sour past
My heart looks for her—it listens for her

Love finds me underneath my speechless tongue
With my eyes closed—hands over my ears
Holding my heart
Love finds me with my faith in my prayer
Asking a love that no matter where we are
You won't let go of my heart

Search

I've searched both near and far
To find the meaning of what you are
At least to me, my reason to live
Words can't express, feelings can't give
The search continues both day and night
You're the guide for my feet
And such a lovely light
My heart does burn for feelings unrevealed
For the heat of passion
Time does stand still
Yet, I'll continue to wait
And travel love's unproven road
For my bittersweet search only you control

Secret Conversation

Love has articulated a conflicting message
Cleverly masking a confident statement
Though contrary to abstract beliefs
Love does not dare speak its name

What authority does love's questions have?
Seeking the all consuming translations of the unknown
Love approaches me in secret- leaving me as an
    opportunity
Conversely, love has saturated my speechless soul

The Music Of The Orchestra

I conduct the orchestra to play
As I place my hand upon your face
Blood flows quickly through the body
The heart pounds like a drum a rhythmic beat
The tone is now set
As thoughts run together
Your lips—the music I desire to sample forever

Like a dance—breathing is done at a quicken pace
Back and forth my eyes move as though searching for a
    place
To kiss your very soul
So—for now I start with your lips—
Music from the orchestra begins to play—your mouth
    parts—
Inviting me to take a sip

With no shame I accept the invitation
I explore the music I've never heard
For me such jubilation

If forever could be captured in a bottle
Then let me seal the bottle tight
For my lips felt the music of the orchestra
When I kissed your lips—goodnight

I Can't Thank You Enough

Thank you for wanting to be there
Thank you for the unheard prayer
Thank you for wishing to send flowers
That somehow never got there

Thank you for the unhappy thoughts
And for the hand that never touched
Thank you for never arriving
Yes, indeed—I thank you much

I thank you for the no hugs
Yes that empty embrace
Thank you for the make believe kisses
That never found my face

Truly I thank you for never trying
To reach me—when you had the breath
And no tears upon my face
Means you thank me in your death

I Owe This To You

I resent the fact that I have but one love to give
For all that love is and all that you are
I'm deeply sadden
That I can love you all that I can
Yet it is still not enough
No fault of yours

To love you is a joy and to be loved by you is an honor
You've given me the courage and the strength
To believe that love does exist
And that it can rest gently on the mind and heart

For this gift I drop to bended knees and thank you
I take great pleasure in knowing
That one of life's most treasured feelings I've conquered
And I owe this to you

When in this world and at this time it seems so easy to
    hate
You make it a moment that's so hard not to love

Pretending

I pretend we never loved
I pretend we never dreamed
I pretend out loud we laughed
I pretend to know what it all means

I'll pretend you never existed
I'll pretend we never cried
I'll pretend shared moments weren't real
I'll pretend
Lord knows I've tried

I'm pretending not to care
I'm pretending there is someone else
I'm pretending not to love you
I'm pretending yet fooling not even myself

If though I stop pretending
And except this reality
I'm afraid my make believe world
Will pretend we shall never be

The Richness Of Mother

Although I was ignorant and poor
My mother loved me dearly
Love is not love she would say
If the love is not from sincerity
Mother was strong in word and mind
She was the one I truly admired
She symbolized love and greatness in one
And of me she never got tired
Poor was mother but she was rich in love
And when I think of my loving mother
I look to the high above
Mother if you can hear me
I pray I make you proud
I'm glad to claim you my mother
And I'm so glad you claimed me your child

Vulnerable Am I

Vulnerable am I to your sun kissed skin
Inducing me to fan my mind's portrait
Of an opium flavor taste
Which requires me to go inside myself
And return tenderhearted
Looking for your moon licked smile
For, as I love you
I know that I love myself
Oh how vulnerable am I to you
Thus so, that when you breathe
It is I, inhaling the life
Which exhales my love for you

Celebration Of Beauty

Tonight I'm arrested by my want of you
Desire please rescue me
From my dream's handcuffs of passion
Tonight love will set me free

Tonight the crackling of candle flames
Keeps blind time
For tonight you are my butterfly
Through your mind I spread your wings
As tonight I make you mine

Tonight there is power in your beauty
Commanding that I give you the air I breathe
Tonight I want to get behind your eyes
And have your love rain down on me

Tonight my kiss speaks of your soft skin, sleek
    shoulders—
And your lips gentle touch
Under the midnight sun I wear love's fabric
While bathing tonight in your love's drinking cup

Tonight in my bed—your thighs will be my banquet
A feast for a king
Tonight my desire's hunger is fed
As tonight I make you my queen

To an acappella tune—tonight my tongue shall dance
     upon the clouds
Then serenade the ear and mouth of this new love I've
     found
Tonight is a celebration of your beauty—forever I shall
     taste your smile
As the memory of this night devours all sound

Tonight I lay in your arms
Making this comfort my home
I place my ear to the ticking clock within you
As night whispers thoughts giving bones a new song

Remembrance of this night
Your love is my love and as we depart
Our love lives within my mind—never leaving my heart

So tonight my hands shall speak of your champagne
     palace, your graceful lines
Your alluring and gentle curves
Tonight I speak only with my eyes
Because tonight you are too beautiful for words

Lost In My Heart

I lost myself in the space of our stare
In the sky's blue face—the sun's steamy glare
Motionless we bring together all parts of us
The hiding public, the open private parts of us
Judgment strings are tenderly severed
Allowing my mind to drift wherever
Suddenly clinging to a runaway cloud
My mind's thoughts are in concert, playing silently loud
How do I ever find my way back to me?
With the gaze of distance eyes not setting me free
A chill runs through vanished moments, time seems to
    disappear
I seek warmth from your eyelids, the cloth I hope to wear
But as you turn and your eyes walk away from me
I accept
In the cold stare of beautiful eyes—what a wonderful
    place to be
Making me feel so close to you this night
When you fall asleep I too close my eyes
So that I might dream of eyes I never knew
Because lost in my heart are my eyes for you

Traveling Love Dream

I left myself in hopes to arrive at your heart
In hopes that your spirit would lead me to the entrance
Of where all love begins
Though deceptive is the unexpected

I follow the path of fallen stars, broken vessels, crumbled
    leaves
Gravity becomes a non-issue as I rise into the air
Hopelessness screams at my steps which are no longer my
    own
My destination reached—so I knock at the door of
    emptiness

The warmth of Hello must have been stolen or escaped
For she knew me not—
In this moment my tongue nor heartbeat seem of no use
    to me
Pain wears no disguise—not even for the ignorance of
    love

Who but I can articulate my reason for leaving self
Intoxicating is my dream of love which taste different
    every night
Yielding a profound sweetness of a non offensive fondness
For a heart that knows me not

I extend my affections toward the obedience of my heart
I search for your heart as though searching for a rose
In the midst of beautiful weeds
Love skews my judgment—remorseful do I become

Tonight I leave myself in hopes that I might arrive at your
    heart
My guiding light is not of you but of an angel's
    outstretched arms
Requesting that I make my bed in heaven amongst the
    stars
So that my dream of love and my long for you won't have
    to travel very far

My Clenched Heart

Her lips and kisses tonight
Belong to the sky
She's embraced in its arms

Tears stain and blind my sight
Clenched heart knows not why
Stars are a glittering charm

I loved her
The way I knew to love
Carefree like the wind

Hidden flower
Sent from the moon above
Loved you without me knowing when

Love unrequited
Leaving a faint perfume
So my kiss is to the sky

Finding her heart committed
By the sky she's consumed
My clenched heart is left open tonight

Opening Speech

Like the want of fire
Is the heart that constantly yearns for more
Knowing nothing but wild abandonment
No attempt to understand
For air cannot follow the trail of the flying dove

How I wish to love you
But like an empty grave you invite me in
And I must not accept
My mind must not ride upon the galloping horse of no
    direction
For passion knows not one heart from another—it burns
    without caring

Never satisfied is my love for you
I give to the greediness of the fire—
My being
And my quest to please—

My passion to love
Runs like an overflowing river
Bursting a heart that yearns to give
Leaning to but one understanding
Which is to love like fire until all is gone

Like Water You Are

Your body is like water to my mouth
Moist love dampening all that it touches
Your slender fingers become melted morsels
Dripping against, slipping through—heated skin
Your arms in silence swallows up everything
Desperate am I for your perfect liquid
To hide myself in your unknown distance
Your feet, your legs—seek ground on airy mountains
Eloquent is my desire—following my tongue
Down the pathway of love—to a newly formed stream
Which invites me to caress my despair
So I drink my fill for hours
While in my head your voice does dance
Your words drive my thirst—each word strokes me
    differently
How irresistible is the drink of passion—
My drink of you—you- my drink of water
Seeping from your watery breath is life
Wildly the horses gallop through my blood
As your sweet lips cover me—like a river of pleasure
Your kisses engulf me—your eyes are lit like stars
They are the flame that dims the moon
How I revel in this water of joy
So much so—that when I place my hands upon your skin
I simply sank everything that is me—into you

About the Author

Keenan Kelly resides in the suburbs of Atlanta, Georgia. He has been writing what he likes to refer to as *"Thought Poetry"* since his early childhood years. These thoughts were simply *"UNINVITED FEELINGS"* that he kept a journal of for his personal enjoyment. Never intending to share his poetry with the world. It was only after receiving encouragement from his family and friends of his unique talent and artistic vision that he decided to publish his works.

He has had several of his poems published by the International Library of Congress. His artistry appears in *"The Rainbow's End,"* a book of anthology and also in the upcoming release of *"The Silence Within."* Keenan was recently inducted into the International Society of Poets and nominated as the 2001 World Champion Amateur Poet.

Keenan is currently working on his next project. Which is assured to enlighten the world with his flair to metaphorically tell the story of life in its entire genre.

0-595-22266-8